# BEST WAYS TO INVEST IN SILVER

## FOR BEGINNERS

## M.L. PILGRIM

# KENOSIS BOOKS: INVESTING IN PRECIOUS METALS SERIES

If you are looking for investment that offers you inflationary protection and that reduces your investment risk significantly, precious metals such as gold, silver, and platinum (amongst others) is the way to go. Unlike paper money, precious metals have a finite supply and you cannot print more of them, and because of this, precious metals offer authentic insurance against political and financial upheavals. This book will share about the ff:

WHAT ARE PRECIOUS METALS?
WHY YOU SHOULD INVEST? - THE UPSIDE AND DOWNSIDE
WHO SHOULD INVEST?
WHAT PRECIOUS METALS SHOULD YOU INVEST IN?
WAYS TO INVEST IN PRECIOUS METALS
CONCLUSION- WHEN SHOULD YOU INVEST?

The primary aim of this eBook is to open young investors' eyes to the infinite possibilities of investment in precious metals. This eBook shows you that you have the time advantage of youth and the ability to take on more risks, and that these advantages can help you make better and bigger investment profits, whether you choose to invest in gold, palladium, copper, silver, or platinum and whether you choose to invest in coins, bars, rounds, or precious metal ETFs.

So take action, and scan the QR CODE and/or Subscribe to our newsletter for more updates!

# BEST WAYS TO INVEST IN SILVER

TO MY WIFE AND MY SON, THIS BOOK IS FOR YOU.

© Copyright 2020 by M. L. PILGRIM - All rights reserved.

Cover Design by Kenosis Book Publishing

ISBN 979-8-5741-8480-6 (Paperback)

The content contained within this book may not be reproduced, duplicated, or transmitted without direct written permission from the author or the publisher.

Under no circumstances will any blame or legal responsibility be held against the publisher, or author, for any damages, reparation, or monetary loss due to the information contained within this book, either directly or indirectly.

Legal Notice:

This book is copyright protected. It is only for personal use. You cannot amend, distribute, sell, use, quote or paraphrase any part, or the content within this book, without the consent of the author or publisher.

Disclaimer Notice:

Please note the information contained within this document is for educational and entertainment purposes only. All effort has been executed to present accurate, up to date, reliable, complete information. No warranties of any kind are declared or implied. Readers acknowledge that the author is not engaged in the rendering of legal, financial, medical, or professional advice. The content within this book has been derived from various sources. Please consult a licensed professional before attempting any techniques outlined in this book.

By reading this document, the reader agrees that under no circumstances is the author responsible for any losses, direct or indirect, that are incurred as a result of the use of the information contained within this document, including, but not limited to, errors, omissions, or inaccuracies.

# Table of Contents

INTRODUCTION ............................................................................... 7
IS INVESTING IN PRECIOUS METALS A GOOD IDEA? ............... 8
WHY SILVER? ................................................................................ 11
ADVANTAGES OF TRADING IN SILVER ..................................... 15
DISADVANTAGES OF TRADING IN SILVER ............................... 18
IS TRADING IN SILVER PROFITABLE? ....................................... 21
HOW TO START THE BUSINESS ................................................. 24
HOW & WHERE TO TRADE SILVER LIKE A PRO ...................... 27
BEST SILVER TRADING STRATEGIES ....................................... 29
CONCLUSION ................................................................................ 32
BONUS Chapter: NICE FEW TIPS AND WARNINGS ................. 33
ABOUT THE AUTHOR M. L. PILGRIM ........................................ 37
BOOKS BY THIS AUTHOR ........................................................... 38
BOOKS BY THIS AUTHOR – S.K. PILGRIM ............................... 49
BOOKS BY THIS AUTHOR – I.K. BUTCHER .............................. 52

# Introduction

I want to thank you and congratulate you for purchasing the book, *"Best Ways to invest in Silver"*.

This book contains proven steps and strategies on how to discover the hidden side of precious metals most especially - silver.

It is known that trade is the most profitable field at all, and what distinguishes it from others is that you can start small in it and grow gradually to become very great. You can penetrate the horizons and exceed your childhood dreams. We all dreamt about successful lives living in a nice place with access to choices that wealth can provide us. How is that? The answer is easy my friend, trade is your best solution.

As the trade has many types, you must specialize in one of them. Most of them are good and will give you a great deal of money, but some may make it happen very quickly and others may be delayed a little. The best trade in our view and in the eyes of many economic analysts is the trade of precious metals such as gold, silver, and so on.

Gold may lead the scene in this regard, but I should draw your attention to the fact that silver is also a very viable option that people may not pay much attention to it. Silver represents a global market with daily changing prices, even if its changes are less severe and violent than gold, they remain variable, and this means that the price movement and its behavior need to be studied. And of course, as a novice investor, you will need some advice so that you do not get lost while you are going on this path. And here comes our turn!

Thanks again for purchasing this book, I hope you will enjoy it!

# Chapter 1
## IS INVESTING IN PRECIOUS METALS A GOOD IDEA?

People from many ages and from various nations have traded in precious metals. No one knows exactly why, but perhaps it is scarce, and given that human nature tends to love ownership and love of being alone with things, the trade in precious metals has grown in popularity and expansion with time. This is indeed true and realistic. Humans love to own something that no one else has, and their pleasure will be much greater if this thing is desired by everyone.

The gold and silver markets, in particular, constitute the largest part of the trade of precious stones around the world due to their relative availability and at the same time their scarcity and average prices, which makes them accessible to buyers around the world. Who does not have anything made of silver or gold in the house?

**Advantages in trading precious metals**

- *A safe haven*

Most of the precious metals are very safe to trade in, especially gold and silver, as they are not affected much by strong economic turns, and even if their price falls a little, it returns to the rise to make a profit in all cases later and in the long term. So, if you ask any gold dealer, the first thing he/she will say to you is that this trade needs patience and anticipation of prices.

But what we would like to say here is that this kind of trade will preserve your capital as much as possible. You may have heard of the fierce battles between gold and real estate, where each of them fights for the title of the safest field ever. If you are one of those people who are afraid of losing their capital, with low entry barrier, then we want to tell you that you have come to the right place.

- *Variety of options*

Contrary to what everyone believes, precious metals trading is not confined to gold. Yes, it is the most famous among them, but it is not the only one at all, this business gives you countless opportunities to trade and a very large number of metals that you can trade with such as silver (it is the most famous and strongest after gold), platinum and palladium and even precious stones are all available for sale and purchase, and the demand for them is increasing.

Not only that, but each of these options includes several other options that you can choose between. For example, gold can be traded as raw gold and you will find many customers for it, and you can also trade it after its manufacture and formation into jewelry for decoration. You can sell bars directly and you can also sell rings, bracelets, necklaces, etc.

- *You determine your business system*

Another advantage that exists in trading in precious metals is the possibility of choosing from many business systems. You can trade in precious metals as a shop or small investor, or you can also trade through investment certificates from banks. Both cases will require roughly the same instructions and the same advice, but the preference is always in favor of the method you are most comfortable with.

Other than these two, there are some other options, but they are somewhat less famous because they merge two types of investment together, but the money return from them is usually large. One of these methods is to buy some shares in companies that trade in metals such as gold and silver, but here you must learn the basics of the stock exchange and how to do technical and fundamental analysis and other principles of trading in the stock exchange. There is another option is to trade gold and silver on forex, but here too you must learn the basics of forex such as analysis, anticipating news, and so on.

## Gold

He is the godfather of this entire family. Gold is known to come to the fore and as a number one if we want to talk about jewelry or even when talking about precious metals in general. It is characterized by several things that make it unique to the fore. The most important of which is that it is never exposed to rust and does not lose its luster over time, it is easy to form and recycle it, it is a good conductor of heat and electricity, too.

It is the basis of the economy of many countries, such as Australia, for example. Indeed, in the very recent past, it was used as an official currency instead of cash. Gold prices change around the clock, every day throughout the year, and there are many online tools that you can use to check the instantaneous price of gold whenever you want. The use of tools like this is necessary when entering any deal, whether buying or selling, and it is even important when buying gold as an adornment. No more so as not to be defrauded.

The demand for gold is increasing day by day, and people's love for this yellow metal may be due to several reasons, including:

- The instability of global conditions at the present time, the confusion of many countries and the confusion of the economy in them, perhaps for this reason you can notice that the price of gold is very high and has even reached its highest levels in decades. As we said before, gold is considered a safe haven for investors to resort to in difficult times
- Inflation, when the prices of all investments rise, and you can choose from several options only a few, so gold is often your best choice.

If you would like to learn more about investing in gold, I have a book entitled "Best Ways to Invest In Gold" and you can read more about this viable investment option. I have shared some description as well in the "Books By This Author" Section.

## Silver

Silver is distinguished from gold in a central thing, which is that the price of silver depends on two factors:

1. the first is the importance of silver as a metal for decoration and jewelry making, and
2. the second is the importance of silver as an important industrial material.

This information may be considered new to you, but what you may not know is your device, of which if you are reading this in eBook format now, whether it is a computer, a phone, or a tablet, has silver strips inside!

In any case, we will talk in detail about silver in the next chapters, so let's prepare ourselves for the sharing that will follow.

The rest of the minerals such as platinum and palladium are classified in the category of industrial minerals and are widely used in factories and commercial activities, so if you are interested in this type of trade, you can think of these minerals. But our book talks in detail about silver, so we will not dwell too much on these minerals.

# Chapter 2
## WHY SILVER?

You may ask yourself while you are reading now, and you may also ask us an important and obvious question: Why silver in particular? We would like to tell you that this topic is carefully selected because it has already proven successful repeatedly with so many people. We have previously provided hundreds of advices in the field of silver trade, and thousands have already benefited from them. We have seen many successful experiences by ourselves, and we decided to publish this book to get you to become one of them, or at least to help you in that. At any rate, this is your decision and yours alone.

**What distinguishes silver from other precious metals**

- *Relatively large availability*

Silver is more popular than you expect, perhaps because you are a non-professional, you will not be very able to differentiate between silver prepared and stainless steel, for example. This is not a problem for you, anyway, as distinguishing between them is really difficult for the sightseeing from afar. But did you know that the spoons in your kitchen may be made of silver when you least expect? Or those utensils in which you eat with daily, many of them are made of silver. Here, I am telling you about the usual household or personal tools that have great daily use.

But if we move to the field of jewelry, silver is very popular around the world, as it is the preferred metal for middle-income earners, because its price is lower than gold and it is very beautiful despite that. In fact, many people, even those with a lot of money, prefer to have silver over gold, not because of its price, but because its appearance is better for them, as you know beauty is relative in everything even here.

- *Average price affordable for most classes of the people*

It is not exclusively for super-rich people like diamonds and not only as well for those with very low incomes like iron and copper, but it is right there in the in the middle cutting across, there where most people can buy it without suffering and without owing money. And yes, there are a lot of people out there who would just borrow money to buy some jewelry (we've seen amazing cases).

You may find some of your relatives or friends among those who prefer the shine of silver or the silver color in general over gold. So, they may like silver more, and if you ask a logical question now about why they do not prefer diamonds because it is close to silver, I will tell you that silver will not be as expensive as diamonds, but it is very similar to its appearance, just as silver has a special luster that can be distinguished from diamonds. True or not, some people prefer Silver luster than the diamond.

This feature will give you great comfort when trading for a good reason, which is targeting a large number of people, meaning that your target audience will be very large, and with this, your sales will increase a lot, especially in popular neighborhoods and markets that people go to a lot. The profit margin in silver trading may be little but the large number of sales will cover significantly for the margins, and the result is a double profit more than that resulting from trading gold or diamonds, you will not believe until you try yourself.

- *Less affected by economic shocks than gold*

As we told you before, gold is considered a safe haven. This is absolutely true and in the opinion of all economic analysts, not only in our opinion. But when we come to silver, the matter is until it becomes safer. I do not remember a global crisis that struck the world before and removed silver from its throne. That is because we had previously said that the price of silver depends mainly on two factors and not one factor. Let's say this more frankly, the main driver of the global silver price is the people's demand for it and its popularity which is increasing day by day.

If you buy silver only for decoration, then you will not pay much attention to this factor, but if you intend to invest in silver, this is undoubtedly the most important factor for you. Any investor puts his priority in preserving capital. And if you want my opinion, this is the right behavior, especially for young people and beginners in the market. New investors are often characterized by recklessness, especially when it comes to trading in precious metals, so do not be a victim of haste and try to find the safest start.

**Do people still buy silver to this day? Why?**

The answer to the first question is clearly yes, people are still racing to buy silver, otherwise we would not have bothered you with this book. As for your question about the reason, we can summarize it as follows:

- *Habit*

Some people, especially in popular or relatively poor neighborhoods, are accustomed to buying and owning silver only because they saw their people do this. I am talking here about very simple people and some of them are also uneducated. So, when someone wants to buy a gift for his lover, sister, daughter, or whatever, the first thing that comes to mind in these areas of the earth is buying silver, gold will look very formal and expensive and diamonds require a lot of money, and copper is never a gift, so silver would seem an ideal middle ground.

- *Wholesalers*

Some merchants may make a quick deal here or there by buying a large amount of a certain form of silver (for example 300 or 400 pieces) at the wholesale price, which will be somewhat cheap, and then they start selling that quantity per piece with a high profit margin to cover the price of storage, delivery, etc. And a small quick note, if you like this idea, we will tell you right away how to implement it in detail. In any case, these merchants often expand little by little until they are able to open a complete business based on silver trade, whether online or in a real store, after they have made a name and reputation for themselves.

- *Some people buy it as jewelry*

As we explained earlier, many people prefer to wear silver over other precious metals. And if you want to succeed in this type of trade, you must be sufficiently intelligent that you can target these people as potential customers when you start your business and start making advertisements for your shop or your site or whatever.

- *Industries*

Most of the machinery and equipment industries include in one of their many stages the use of silver. Some economists even refer to silver as the industrial metal due to its penetration into many industrial fields, and here we are not talking about plates or spoons. We are talking about computers, mobile phones and even cars! Silver offers some kind of unique physical properties cheaper than its peers. So, if someone thinks about starting a factory or establishing a brand for a new industrial company, he must allocate a budget for silver alone.

## Real world example, happening right now!

During the time of this writing, we are in 2020, witnessing a painful global blow to the entire global economy by this Covid-19 pandemic. All commodities have decreased and have not decreased before, even salaries and the value of the currency. All these things are affected, and some countries have almost declared bankruptcy. But do you know what remained resilient in the face of the storm? Almost the only element that, unlike the rest of them, increased in price and did not decline or even maintain the price, gold and silver, why? As we said before because they are a safe economic haven.

# Chapter 3
## ADVANTAGES OF TRADING IN SILVER

There is a golden rule that can be followed in any type of project, and by that I really mean anything from small craftsmanship to creative professions such as writing, photography, and drawing, to our topic today, which is trade.

The main factor that will encourage you to start your business is your vision of the results on the ground. Your vision of this project and that it has already succeeded and increased the income of many, so you will automatically want to be one of them.

Even this principle is well known in psychology, and many parents follow it in rearing their children. If you want your son to get used to a certain habit or to make him move away from a bad habit, then it is better than to punish him nor shout at him nor even advise him in a direct way is to allocate a reward to him whenever he does this good behavior or whenever he moves away from bad behavior.

This is the so-called principle of reward, and the same thing is followed in business. Your heart will not be reassured unless you see examples that have actually preceded you and succeeded in the same field of business.

Here, when we talk about the silver trade, it is sufficient for you to go to one of the stores near your house and sit with the seller for a half hour, no more, to be reassured.

You can ask him / her if the field is profitable and if it is enough to create a full life, and even if it is sufficient when you can reach this stage. Also, ask him/her when you can reach full financial freedom. You will find it worth thinking about. Of course, we can give you the answers, but as we said a little while ago, the most important thing is to be completely reassured. Also, just note that if they have been long into the business, definitely, your answer will be a resounding "Yes" but be prepared to here the advices and tips as well from them – as long as you can assure them that you will not go direct competition with them.

**Advantages of silver trading in this decade**

- *You will trade in tangible things that are immortal*

Yes, as I just said it, immortal. The most important and biggest advantage of trading silver is that it is a sensory commodity that you can carry in your hand and act with it however you want. If you are one of the people who do not feel very comfortable when trading in the stock exchange or in the stock market because they do not have the commodities in their hands, we would like to tell you that you will be very comfortable in this kind of trade. Also, silver is easy to carry, light in weight and gives great freedom to its owner regarding carrying, transportation and storage.

Another thing is that silver is simply not perishable. They cannot be burned (*Of course it can be melted, but this is done under special conditions with tools specially made for such situations and this often happens in laboratories rather than in the usual stores*) and cannot be broken easily. Silver does not rust. Therefore, you can store it for years and nothing will happen to it, so it is on the list of the top 10 trading businesses in the long term.

- *One of the easiest goods to store*

As a beginner in the field of trade, you will probably be a little anxious about the storage process simply because you do not know much about it and do not have sufficient experience for it, and indeed one of the most problems that impede new merchants that they complain to us because of it is storage. All you will need in this topic is a medium-sized, simple safe that you can put in your home or office or even store it with a reliable shipping company if you intend to sell by piece online.

In the event that a new silver store is opened, the storage becomes easier and easier. You will need that same safe, but smaller in size, to store the excess goods or large quantities of a particular piece and the basic commodities you will place in the store to become in front of the visitors' eyes so that they can see and examine them well. And here we will give advice that may seem intuitive, but a lot are actually missing it. Do not tell anyone the password to the safe and keep it well.

- *A trade that does not depend much on technology*

Just as technology has facilitated everything and even the silver trade, and no one can object to this, it has some disadvantages as well. It is true that it is not many and it is not very influential, but it still exists. When you open an electronic store or a website to sell products on the Internet, here you are competing with a very large number of merchants.

Of course, the more competition intensifies, the more difficult it will be for beginners, because you not only compete with beginners like you, but also compete with large merchants who have great experience in the field and know its secrets and tricks that enable them to sell large quantities in a short time. That may reduce the number of your customers because they would prefer someone with a name and a brand because he/she would be more reliable.

The advantage here in silver is that if you see this matter as a major obstacle or something that may stand in your way at the beginning, you can stay away from all of this and limit your competition to two or three stores in your neighborhood and the nearby neighborhood as well! It's really that simple, and you will find many customers without the need for intense advertising campaigns, views, followers, etc. All you will have to do is to learn the principles and basics of selling just to be able to deal with customers well and make them love and trust your store, and thus they will prefer it when buying.

- *Trade without fear of contracts*

Another thing that you will not feel its value until after testing it is that the silver trade is often an individual trade, meaning that you go to buy the commodity or silver pieces that you will sell on your own and you will store it on your own and you will also sell it on your own without any partners, contracts, or penalty terms.

This does not mean that you will never work alone, but those whom you will work with will be co-workers who take a salary from you for their work and not partners. This will give you a lot of latitude.

Hundreds of businesses are closed daily due to the termination of contracts or the lack of agreement between the partners, which forces one of the parties to resort to the court, and the matter may reach imprisonment or a fine if one of the parties is unable to pay the penalty clause or pay his / her debt, if any. The silver trade takes you out of all this safely and free to do whatever you want with your merchandise.

- *Huge number of suppliers*

The silver market includes a large number of local and international suppliers, this variety of options when choosing a supplier will provide you with your goods at the cheapest possible price. There are many trade methods that obligate you to only one seller or supplier and therefore you cannot negotiate much with him / her on the price, but here while you are trading in silver you will find in front of you a remarkable difference in prices and you can then ask each merchant separately on the advantages that he provides and then choose the best option for you.

# Chapter 4
## DISADVANTAGES OF TRADING IN SILVER

You might think for a moment, if the silver trade is so perfect as you say, why not all people trade in it? On the contrary, we do not find many silver traders, such as gold traders, for example. Don't worry, we don't want to harm you, we just want to help. It is true that gold trading is more common than silver, but this does not necessarily mean that silver trading is bad.

Let me simplify the matter for you a little before going into the details of the flaws of silver trade (*Yes, we will not complain about you, and we will tell you about the problems or difficulties that you may face, but we will also tell you how to solve them*). But for clarification, let me give you an example. If you ask a random group of 100 people, for example, about their preferences between apples and oranges, if we bear in mind that apples are really the most popular and most beloved fruit in the world, you will find that most people have chosen apples.

But does this mean that oranges are bad? Or is the orange less useful than apples? No, it is only the preferences and comfort of traders for one type of trade over another. Of course, you would not base your decision on trade on merely preferences, would you? But with all the love for orange, it also has drawbacks, as it is relatively hard to peel and tastes a bit sour.

So, let's now start by mentioning the factors that make many people away from the orange trade, I mean silver, sorry!

**Disadvantages of silver trading in the decade**

- *Using it only in jewelry*

Many experts advise that if you start trading in silver, or at least make this decision, you should diversify your options slightly and not limit them to selling jewelry for women. Of course, selling jewelry is one of the most famous if not the most popular use of silver in the last few years, but also putting all your hopes on this element only will put you in some danger, and as we said before, make your safety of your investment your priority.

To trade in decorations, jewelry and this classification, you here depend entirely on the taste of your customers. But it is dangerous to think that your tastes or the shapes that you have chosen will necessarily be chosen by them. Here, you may bear the cost of a large number of silver jewelry, and then you cannot sell them easily, and with time these shapes will be presented or their price will decrease, and therefore even if you do not bear losses you will not make a profit.

The solution here may be divided into two parts, the first is very logical, as long as your business, in this case, depends on the tastes of the people around you, why not you offer them different shapes first before you buy a quantity of them and then analyze the opinion poll that you did. Based on specific figures and unmistakable analyses, you can buy a large amount of the product that the audience likes! You can do these polls also on Facebook, Twitter, Instagram and of course the popular one, Pinterest. You can engage in groups and various forums online and learn more about the popular ones and most sellable.

The other solution is to diversify your investment a little, and to put that in a rather simple sense, we will assume that we have a ring of gold, for example, or diamonds, but we want to add another color to it for a more attractive shape or for an innovative idea that may attract the attention of customers. Here we can use some silver strips and combine them with these materials to produce us a masterpiece. What we are simply saying is that you expand your thinking to be able to bring out your best and not stick to just one form of trade.

- *Silver bank bond*

One of the problems you may face, especially if you love this type of trade is this. This problem is divided into two parts. The first is that bank bonds for silver are not widespread and are not available in many banks, so you may face some difficulty in finding the right deal, but you can always resort to the Internet solution and buy bank bonds in international banks with the click of a button while you are sitting in your place.

The second part of the problem is that even if you find bank notes of silver in your town somehow, it will be difficult to find them at the same price as silver in the market. The same applies to gold, by the way, for this you do not hear much about gold trading through bank bonds, and often the people who resort to this method are those who want to invest in the long term.

- *Income is not fixed*

This may be a general problem in all types of trade, but it becomes a little clear when trading precious metals. The reason for this is somewhat logical, people buy gold and silver as gifts or to adorn them with nothing more, so all these beautiful rings and bracelets are classified as luxuries and not essential to life.

What if exposing people to financial hardship? What do you think is the first thing people will think of doing without to save their financial situation? I think the answer is clear now, of course they will try to dispense with the luxuries and the first thing they will think about is that silver and gold will not end in the world, so we will not buy now and when our financial situation becomes better, we will buy then it is okay. And if you want my opinion, this thinking is correct.

Therefore, we always say that global crises do not clearly reduce the price of silver directly, but they still affect it indirectly. When a global crisis or an economic crisis occurs, people will lose a lot of money, so they will not pay attention to something that will not make a big difference in their lives, such as jewelry.

However, in light of crises, silver shines more than gold, because the wealthy class of the people will still be affected, but they will be able to buy anyway, and in this situation they will not go to buy gold for its expense, so who comes as one number in the options offered? Absolutely yes, silver.

And if you want more safety, we can bring you back to advice that also applies to all categories of trade, namely, the establishment of an emergency fund. This surplus money will protect you from violent shocks in the market that may push many traders to shut down the entire business. It would be great if you saved at the beginning of your career and then saved the money in anticipation of any personal or economic circumstances.

# Chapter 5
## IS TRADING IN SILVER PROFITABLE?

If all of what was previously mentioned is not enough to convince you, let me give you an example from history. Do you hear about the pharaohs? The maid of those Egyptians who live in Africa. Many around the world say they are one of the greatest if they are not really the greatest people in history. They introduced things that even today, even with all this technology, no one can offer. Do you know what their currency was? Gold and silver.

Not because they could not create a special currency, but because they knew the value of these minerals. You can open google now and search for the tombs of the ancient pharaohs. Do not be afraid, they are not usual graves, but are made of pure gold, because they believe that they will live again in another world and thus bury their possessions with them in order to remain rich in the afterlife.

No one throughout history has not realized the value of precious metals, so do not question them now, and we will list to you the reasons that make silver in particular and precious metals in general worthy of investment and placing confidence in them.

**But I am still worried about this area after all this!**

If you still think that way, that's okay, that's completely normal. Any trader should feel anxious at first, especially if the market he / she will enter is relatively small, such as the silver market. The investment decision is indeed a difficult decision, but after a while you will realize that it was the best decision in your life. But to be honest, it may sometimes be a wrong decision, but that is only in the case of haste and not studying the matter seriously.

**Reasons for the possibility of making a huge profit from the silver trade**

- *At the end of the day, silver is still real money*

Gold and silver, even if they are not used as official currencies, they remain a form of money. They are literally money. By buying gold or silver, you are only converting the image of the money that you own from cash to precious metals that are safer and less turbulent. Our talk here is about physical silver, not ETFs, investment certificates, or even stock exchange.

This can all be summarized by saying that silver is a storage of value only until its price increases, then you can sell to get a profit. This is a bit like trading currencies, but in a much safer way.

- *A global currency that you can trade anywhere in the world*

One of the most important advantages that can rain dollars on you is that the price of silver is uniform and global in any country. The price of silver is renewed around the clock in all parts of the world. The price of silver in India is the same as the price of silver in the United States, for example.

How does this benefit you? Simply you can create an online store to display your goods not only for the neighborhood you live in, not even your city only, but for the entire world. In this case, you will need to contract with an international shipping company to deliver your orders to the customers' home without problems, damage, or loss of the goods.

- *Silver is simply cheap*

This project won't cost you much at first, maybe $ 1000 will suffice. Yes, the matter is that simple, so you will not risk much, and when you return again to psychology, we will find that people act better or make better decisions when there is no great pressure on them or when they act in a way free of fear with moderation.

Also, its cheap price and elegant shape make an irresistible mixture for people when they think about gifts. When you open your store one day, you will be dazzled by the looks of people buying gifts for their loved ones, despite their simplicity.

- *Owning silver is much more practical than owning gold or cash*

We explained before that we do prefer owning precious metals over having cash, and it is safer. Now we will tell you about a small feature in which silver greatly outperforms gold. Silver can be bought and sold to give you cash when needed more freely than gold. So, you can sell a small or large amount according to your need, unlike gold, which may sometimes need to sell less than the amount you sell and cannot because that is the least amount that the merchant will accept.

Also, when you own gold jewelry, you will not be able to divide it into parts and you will have to sell it all, although you will not need the full amount, but since the price of silver is cheap, you can sell your silver jewelry per piece, i.e. one or two, to fulfil your need only without any extra money, which will be a loss if the price of silver is bearish. And a small note, if you are thinking about trading silver, always consider silver coins.

- *Silver surpasses gold in the bullion market ... a surprise, isn't it?*

In fact, the silver market is so small that changes occur in it very slowly, and when the word "slow investment" comes to mind, first and foremost the word "long-term investment" should come to your mind, and this word in our current context means bullion. All figures and statistics indicate an overwhelming superiority of silver over gold in terms of bullion trade revenues (about four times the profit in the period between 2008 and 2011 only)

Many governments have stopped manufacturing silver ... It may sound like bad news at first glance but read on!

Perhaps only the United States, India and Mexico are producing silver at the moment. Perhaps the reason is that currencies are not made of silver anymore, and it may be due to the fact that governments at the present time intend to direct their entire stock of silver to the industrial sector, where it is used frequently and necessary for the exit of the final product.

Remember what we said in the beginning of the book? The rarer the silver, the higher its price, and thus you, as a silver merchant, will benefit from the fact that you already own quantities of it that you previously bought at a much cheaper price.

- *The industrial sector is calling you*

Always go in the direction of the wave. If you see the entire market drifting towards the industry, why not start your silver trade with merging into the industrial field? You can address the factories, communicate with them, and link them with silver merchants and suppliers, and take the commission in exchange for coordinating shipping, receiving goods, and so on. Or you can create your own mini factory to make silver plates and spoons, for example, or even picture frames and simple silver artifacts.

# Chapter 6
## HOW TO START THE BUSINESS

One of the things that everyone can agree on is that the beginning is always the hardest thing in general. At the beginning of anything, you do not reap any fruits, you just get tired when you put the seeds in the soil. You usually face many problems, you do not feel enough stimulation, and the biggest problem is that you lose your passion as a result of successive failed attempts. So, if you cross that first stage of anything you want to learn, you will most likely be a professional in it to a large degree, perhaps even more than you had hoped.

Therefore, one of the most important advice that we can give you is not to make the beginning disappoint you, and we are here anyway to show you the best way to start to save yourself a lot of time, money, fatigue and thinking. Silver trading in general is not difficult but it will be easier and smoother with some advice arising from experience.

**Tips for a safer start**

- *Decide what route to take*

In the beginning, you have to answer an important question, which is: Do you intend to trade in silver in the short or long term? The answer to a question like this requires some study first of your capital that you own at the present time, then you try to link this capital with the expected profits and the profits you want to obtain. If you are in a hurry to profit, do not risk a large amount of money and start a small project in the short term.

Another important question is: Will you trade in gold only, or in gold and silver together, or will you add some precious stones and other precious metals? Let me tell you frankly that the answer to such a question may not only be subject to your desire, but rather it will return to the preferences of the audience you target or who live next to you. If your target market is rich and includes money owners, add gold to silver and you will trade better.

A final question that you should ask is: Will you trade only at the local level and make do with making a name and reputation among the people you know and trust, or do you have the ability to move to the global level? You should be aware that an international store is definitely a big step, but it is a bit risky and requires good thinking and scrutiny before starting it so that you do not waste your money amid all these deals that happen online daily.

- *If you choose to trade through stocks or forex, learn the analysis well*

Analysis is the basis of any trading or trading on the Internet, and the advantage that some trading platforms may offer at the present time is to provide an opportunity to experiment with virtual capital to evaluate what you have learned from the analysis and whether you are really able to enter this market or not, so as a preliminary advice you should take All your time learning both technical and classical analysis.

- *Study all options and take your time. Nobody is running after you!*

You can take into account stocks as well as bank bonds, don't exclude them completely at first just because you are worried about them. Try to learn more about them. Research, ask for expert opinions, get to know. Joining forums or groups that discuss this will highly improve your knowledge. For example, some people in those groups will ask questions you never thought of, but those questions will be very much helpful to you.

- *Take the opinion of an experienced financial advisor*

Experienced people always provide support and always enjoy helping small traders, so do not ever feel embarrassed to seek help from large traders and do not think that they will embarrass you or something like that. You can find these experts on silver trade websites or on private groups on Facebook and Instagram. Go to someone and politely ask that he / she give you advice he / she would like if someone gave it to him / her at the beginning, and you will find him / her happy because you put your trust in him / her.

You also have a magic solution to all your problems, but it will be a little costly, to appoint a financial advisor for you to take over all aspects of the work, but even if you resort to this option, try to learn from it and not hold him / her responsible and then turn your back only. Try to ask him / her why he made this decision or why this is the best and why he did not choose another option, for example, with time you will find yourself able to take over the responsibility of your business completely without help.

- *Set your goals before starting to trade*

It is very important to set a goal in the short term, whether this goal is a certain amount of profits or a certain number of customers. Close targets will always encourage you and protect you from falling victim to laziness and despair, and these factors are the most harmful factors that harm small traders. The long-term goals are also very important, because they define the path for you to follow so that you will not be distracted later.

# Chapter 7
## HOW & WHERE TO TRADE SILVER LIKE A PRO

Since silver is not in circulation a lot among traders, it makes it take a somewhat small space in the portfolio of all traders. As numbers, we can tell you that the total value of silver and its investments around the world in 2020 amount to 540 billion dollars, and this number even if you feel that it is a bit large, but it is small, especially when compared to the total value of gold investments, which amount to $ 3.8 trillion!

Half of this silver is allocated to industry and the other half goes to all other investments. It is rare for this value to rise suddenly, which gives the market stability. On the other hand, technically speaking, there are 19.2 billion ounces of silver equivalent to that amount of money, which may give you an idea of the low price of silver compared to other precious metals.

You can notice that we started listing numbers when you started reading about the professional chapter! Therefore, there are some tips that may put you on the first path to professional silver trading.

- *Understand the so-called price chain of silver*

A chain consists of several parts linked together by a thin rope that makes it hold together, right? This is exactly the case here with the price chain. Let's say at the beginning that silver is not affected much by the movements of the stock market until the US stock exchanges, but does this mean that you can completely neglect the stock market operator during your trading? Of course, not.

Silver is heavily affected by gold, and gold, in turn, is greatly affected by the stock market. Therefore, the stock market may not directly affect silver, but it certainly affects it indirectly, and it must be taken into account when trading (you do not have to learn to trade the stock exchange, but only the basics suffice.

- *The best silver traders are those who do not depend on silver only!*

Diversifying your portfolio is a somewhat professional task and you will reach it when you have a lot of experience in the market. But we want you to acquire it now and start applying it early to take a previous step before all other traders. If possible, do not put all your money in silver, you can resort to gold a little, or diversify between forms of silver trade and so on.

- *Watch the dollar price from afar*

Although the effect of the dollar price is slightly weak on silver, it also affects it indirectly, as it affects other factors that affect the price of silver. The general rule is that a decrease in the value of the dollar means an increase in the value of precious metals, including gold and silver, and vice versa. Simply because this means that people are losing their confidence in banks and turning a little toward safer solutions.

## Where can you trade and sell silver?

- *Create your own store*

It is the traditional method, and in my opinion, the most effective. You will need to do some government procedures and obtain licenses for you. If you live in the United States or the United Kingdom and Europe in general, it will only take you a few days. Choose a good niche and use the marketing tools wisely to let your target market know about you.

- *Create an online store*

This is also one of the easy solutions, and if you will resort to this option, start the store on a local scale only, and if you see that you have gained enough experience, you can then consider opening an international online store.

- *Social Media*

If you have a page on social media that includes a large number of followers, you can offer your goods on it and you will initially find a small number of customers, but people interested in your field will start to look at you after each period and another.

- *Connect with factories*

An option that may seem a bit strange and unfamiliar, but it is smart and out of the box. If you have previously worked on this book that the silver market is trending towards industrialization, why not take advantage of this? Contact the factory owners and offer them to provide the silver material they will need at the wholesale price, then contact a supplier to arrange the order.

# Chapter 8
## BEST SILVER TRADING STRATEGIES

If something goes haphazardly, it is often completely destroyed, whether in commerce or any other field. Even if everything goes well for a while, it will not take long for everything to collapse. As you see randomness means gambling, you tried it and succeeded by chance, so your instinct will push you to try it again without awareness, and I do not think that you want to gamble on your head.

There are many silver trading strategies that are simple, easy, and beginner friendly. There are other complex strategies that depend on mathematical operations and numbers. Perhaps the book will not suffice to explain them, and there is the last type of strategies that depend on overlapping with other markets such as the stock market and forex.

But in any case, we will show you the two most popular strategies for trading silver at the present time, namely trading by following the trend and trading by the range. These strategies depend on several factors, the most important of which are:

- *Determine the current market direction.*
- *Determine the market trend in previous years and months.*
- *Expect market movement in the coming months.*
- *Read price signals.*
- *Linking political and economic events to trade.*

**Trend Trading**

In this method, you will open the chart for silver on any website that provides it on the Internet and follow the movement of the silver price in the past few weeks. If you find that the price has been declining for a while and then suddenly becomes in an upward curve and continued for several days, then this may tell you that this is the beginning of an uptrend, and you can then ride the wave and buy silver, whether online or in reality.

On the contrary, I saw the trend was up for a while, then it started to break down and the trend towards the downside. Here you are faced with two options. If you have already entered into a purchase deal, now is the most appropriate time to sell and make profits, and if you have not entered into a deal yet, you can enter it online only because it allows you to sell silver while you do not own it.

We warn that you do not trade in the opposite of the trend or expect it to break and reverse the price without sufficient signals. Wait for it to reverse and begin to countermove. Yes, you will lose some dollars, but it is better than losing all of your money. Study signals well in order to always be on the lookout for price action. Again, these are just some tips and you will be the best to decide when and how much to trade.

**Range Trade**

It is a slightly advanced method than the trend method and depends on determining the range in which the price moves, which requires observing the price in previous times. Determine the areas from which the price rebounds, whether this retracement is up or down, and draw a line at this area. With this process repeated several times, you will find that the price is actually moving within a range that may be up, down, or horizontal.

This way, you can expect that when the price reaches the limits of this range, it will rebound and from here you can enter into a trade. But beware of breaches, as the price may breach the boundaries of the range to continue its movement, which is often a strong movement and lasts for a long time. So, it would be a lot better if you wait to see whether the price has rebounded or broken through the range.

In both methods, you can use the price of gold because it precedes silver, and thus it may give you an estimate of the next direction for silver, but this is not a strategy in itself and you cannot rely on the price of gold to trade silver, but it is only a helpful factor.

**Factors that determine the price of silver in the world**

It is important to know these factors at your start so that you can adapt to the market and simulate international prices so as not to create a gap between your prices and the prices of the competing stores, and you lose your customers. You must be flexible when setting prices for your products and take into account the conditions of the physical region, whether locally or internationally.

- *Silver supply and demand*

You should always follow the daily news about silver in all parts of the world and the positions of governments towards it, and whether the market is moving now, or it is still in a recession. In general, the supply and demand for any commodity whose price is determined greatly. If the demand increases, the price increases, and if the demand decreases, the price decreases. This is one of the general rules for trade and vice versa with supply.

- *Supply and demand for the remaining precious metals*

The rest of the metals, such as gold and platinum, determine the price of silver significantly because they all fall under the same name, which is precious metals. If the price of gold is low, then this means a relative decrease in the price of silver, and if the price of gold increases, the price of silver rises slightly. Of course, there are exceptions to the rule, but in normal circumstances, precious metals increase in price and fall together.

- *Industrial conditions of the state*

If the country is moving towards reviving the industrial field, which in turn is one of the ways to revive the entire economy, then you should know that the price of silver is on the way to rise, and you may have to buy now before the factories withdraw large quantities of silver from the market and thus its price rises a little suddenly.

- *The general economic situation of the country and the whole world. We have already explained this point.*

Again, there are many factors for this but the key message here is that please make sure that you watch the silver price very closely and how it reacts to such changes in the market. When I say how, I don't only refer to the magnitude of the rise and fall of the price, but also on how quick or how sensitive it is. Start small, learn, repeat, and try bigger trades.

# Conclusion

Thank you again for purchasing this book!

I hope this book was able to help you to find your way to your investment road, as we helped you to discover a real hidden treasure.

The next step is to use our advices in the best possible way that can guarantee you success.

Now don't stop there, open your browser, search for more and more tips and strategies. Reading a lot about the topic will make you more familiar if not memorize these methods and encourage you to take this step.

The best time to start anything is not yesterday nor tomorrow. The best time is always today – right at the moment you finish reading the book. In front of you is a great opportunity to make fantastic profits with little effort and in a field that many do not know anything about, so try to seize it.

We wholeheartedly think that we have already provided you with everything you will need in the beginning and even as a professional.

We hope in the near future that you will contact us to inform us that you have already started trading and are making profits from it. Nothing in the world will please us more than that, with our wishes for you good luck and good luck.

Finally, if you enjoyed this book, then I'd like to ask you for a favor, would you be kind enough to leave a review for this book? It'd be greatly appreciated!

Thank you and good luck!

# BONUS Chapter
## NICE FEW TIPS AND WARNINGS

Finally, we would like to tell you some tips and answers that you may need during your journey, especially at the beginning. These tips are the result of the most common questions among merchants in this field, which are directed to us daily. Here we have reached the end of our journey. So put your back well and read these tips and warnings carefully.

- *Select one strategy to work with ... but try more*

If you intend to start, you have to try yourself and not apply what others have done literally because he may simply understand a particular strategy better, or you may possess another type of skill that will enable you to better master another type of strategy. Why do you deny yourself this? There are many platforms that provide you with a free virtual trading experience in silver, register for one of them and apply more than one strategy until you master one.

The most important thing here is that if you settle on a certain strategy, stick to it completely. Even if you lose once or twice, adjust your mistakes, and do not alter the whole strategy, because that will only distract your thinking. If your thinking wanders while you are trading in anything, not just silver, you will definitely lose.

- *Set your budget, do not skimp, and do not overstate*

Do not start with all your capital, start with only about 20% of it as a maximum. This may seem a little inconsequential, but it is more secure, because any business in the world, no matter how good it is, is liable to lose. And if you happen to lose, you may regret a lot if you put your whole money in this area alone.

At the same time, do not enter a small amount or less than $ 1000 because you will not be able to stand on your feet in the market with such a small capital, you will need a lot of money to spend on marketing, for example, and without it your business will be affected.

- *Choose the type of silver you will trade in*

There are two basic types preferred by traders are silver bars and silver coins. To trade in both types is stressful, but it is possible and not impossible, but in the beginning you cannot do this, you will divide your thinking and focus into two halves and thus you will not focus completely on what you are doing. This dual trade needs years of experience and familiarity with the market, competitors, and prices.

- *Choose the broker that you deal with carefully if you choose the online trade route*

The broker that you contract with must be trustworthy, and this can be confirmed by taking the opinions of clients who have dealt with him before, and he must have a name and a position in the market. Beware of this point because many people may fall victim to fraud in this step because they are not able to distinguish good from bad broker. You should also choose the design that suits you the most and that you are comfortable with, after making sure of all this, you will be ready to register and start.

- *Estimate your loss and don't rule it out completely*

Estimating and studying potential loss is very important when starting a business. As we said, no business is 100% secure. So, you must try to provide a safe environment yourself. Take the worst possibilities into consideration and put some plans to get out of the dilemmas that you may face so that you do not get confused and collapse your investment. Planning is the best way to save an investment early.

- *It is better to learn to know the real silver from the fake*

If we are talking about gold, I can put some methods that will help you to distinguish between real and fake gold on your own and easily, but when talking about silver, my advice is to go to a shop that specializes in silver to find out for himself. Detection of real silver requires equipment and devices to produce an accurate result.

Autonomous and traditional methods have become famous for their ineffectiveness, and if you want to buy silver detectors on your own, there is nothing wrong with that, but we may not recommend this step very much at the beginning because it will cost you while you are in need of money. Also, in the beginning, you will not have hundreds of deals that you would like to verify, so it is sufficient to take a random sample from your deal and verify it.

Traditional methods include:

- *Smell it, silver does not smell.*

- *Test it with a magnet, silver is not attracted to a magnet.*

- *Scrub it on a piece of cloth, the silver will not leave a trace on the cloth.*

- *Find the stamp of manufacture to learn the place of manufacture and the type of silver.*

But all of these properties are common to silver and many metals, so it would be better if you stick to our first advice and go to a specialist in metal detection.

# KENOSIS BOOKS: INVESTING IN PRECIOUS METALS SERIES

If you are looking for investment that offers you inflationary protection and that reduces your investment risk significantly, precious metals such as gold, silver, and platinum (amongst others) is the way to go. Unlike paper money, precious metals have a finite supply and you cannot print more of them, and because of this, precious metals offer authentic insurance against political and financial upheavals. This book will share about the ff:

WHAT ARE PRECIOUS METALS?
WHY YOU SHOULD INVEST? - THE UPSIDE AND DOWNSIDE
WHO SHOULD INVEST?
WHAT PRECIOUS METALS SHOULD YOU INVEST IN?
WAYS TO INVEST IN PRECIOUS METALS
CONCLUSION- WHEN SHOULD YOU INVEST?

The primary aim of this eBook is to open young investors' eyes to the infinite possibilities of investment in precious metals. This eBook shows you that you have the time advantage of youth and the ability to take on more risks, and that these advantages can help you make better and bigger investment profits, whether you choose to invest in gold, palladium, copper, silver, or platinum and whether you choose to invest in coins, bars, rounds, or precious metal ETFs.

So take action, and scan the QR CODE and/or Subscribe to our newsletter for more updates!

# ABOUT THE AUTHOR

M. L. Pilgrim lost millions when he was starting as an entrepreneur but only his consistent belief in the power of the subconscious mind has brought him to his success. He is very active investing with majority of his portfolio in precious metals and stocks. Also, he invests in bonds, mutual funds, UITFs, and in other businesses in real estate, power generation, banking, logistics, retail, and telecommunications.

He worked across 10 countries always fascinated with the beauty of nature, culture, and traditions. He is a versatile author writing both fiction and non-fiction. He is a traveler, a dedicated father, a loving son, and a responsible brother.

He strongly believes that everyone can succeed both in business, relationships, society, and other aspects if they only have the right information and knowledge on how to use that information properly.

M. L. Pilgrim uses a pen name as he doesn't want to show himself as a definitive expert. Instead, he is in this journey with his readers like a "pilgrim" and wants to travel with them and share their experiences.

Reach M. L. Pilgrim in mlpilgrim.author@gmail.com. Cheers!

Or subscribe to his newsletter for latest updates on his investment books.

# BOOKS BY THIS AUTHOR

Best Ways to Invest in Gold For Beginners: Quick Guide for Learning and Investing in Gold. (BONUS: 14 Ways to Establish Real Gold from Fake Gold and more!)

*Gold has kept a great value for thousands of years, and until this day it still occupies this high position, due to its properties that make it at the forefront of precious metals.*

As it still retains its value throughout the ages, and the belief that is embedded in people's minds is that gold is the only way to pass and conserve wealth from one generation to another.

In times of political and economic tension as well as natural disasters, investors resort to buying gold as a safe haven in the markets and as a store of value, and it is also used as a hedge against high inflation. If you want gold to be part of your investment portfolio, you can choose from several investment options in gold, each of which has different investment characteristics. In this book, we offer many ways to invest in gold, tips to make the greatest possible start and the guide by which you can avoid fraud. We hope that we could help you, best of luck!

**How to Understand The Subconscious Mind: Unlock, Unleash, and Let it Transform You!**

*What do you know about the subconscious mind?*

*Do you want to know more about its characteristics? It is within us, but it is elusive in many aspects. So, careful understanding of the subconscious mind will bring us many benefits.*

This book will share about the ff:

- What is the subconscious mind?
- Its relationship with the conscious mind
- Methods of connecting with the subconscious mind
- Secrets of the subconscious mind
- The rules of the subconscious mind
- Using your subconscious mind to achieve your goals
- Programming the subconscious mind
- How to achieve sleep miracles
- Controlling your subconscious mind

So, what are you waiting for? Check out this informative yet insightful book in unleashing this mysterious power within ourselves.

How to Thrive in Awkward Conversations: Learn the Art of Speaking with Skill and Consideration (BONUS! 10 TIPS TO IMPROVE YOUR CONVERSATION SKILLS!)

*Have you ever found yourself in the middle of an Awkward Conversation?*

Conversation is an art of dealing and communicating with others. Effective Communication aims to build understanding and acceptance - not conflict. However, there is that other type of conversation - *the awkward conversation.*

When you are in the midst of an embarrassing moment, you see yourself in a situation you wished you were not. Hence, knowing what to do exactly in those moments will prepare you for the worst.

This book will help you on the ff:
- Importance of Speaking Tactfully
- What makes conversations awkward and how to avoid them?
- How to have perfect conversation with your partner?
- How to handle a conversation with your parents?
- Business and work conversations
- General Tips and Tricks to be a top speaker

Grab a copy of this book and start your journey into more assertive, confident, and tactful!

How to Say No to Yourself: Conquering Intermittent Fasting 101-
The #1 Complete Guide for Beginners & Busy People (Bonus: No-
Stress 30-Day Simple Plan, Meal Preparations, Cookbook and more!)

*Intermittent fasting is currently one of the most popular health and fitness trends in the world. It will teach you the unique process of following alternative fasting and feeding cycles.*

This book contains proven steps and strategies on how to intermittently fast for weight loss and also examines the concept of clean nutrition.

By reading it, you will learn practical and proven arts and practices that, if followed religiously, will create a young, vibrant, exuberant, radiant and totally different being.

Do you have to lose weight? Are you trying to adapt to that new outfit for the summer? But you don't want to fall in love with those diets and lose weight with the quick tricks of the past, you need something that really stands the test of time. Much more than a diet, you need a change in lifestyle. This is exactly what the 30-day intermittent fasting challenge offers. Intermittent fasting can restart and restore the body, helping to put metabolic processes back on track. Fasting teaches your body to burn fat instead of complex carbohydrates.

With your body poised and ready to burn fat for fuel, stubborn fatty deposits like your belly, arms and legs will evaporate quickly! It may sound too good to be true, but only by regulating the body through a dedicated and consistent fasting regimen - this is truly possible! This book provides you with the knowledge, background, and recipes to successfully perform your intermittent fasting regime over the course of 30 days.

In this book you will get:
Why fast?
What is intermittent fasting?
Intermittent fasting and your hormones
Intermittent fasting and weight loss
Eat Healthily
The Keto diet
Autophagy and intermittent fasting
Pagan's diet
Intermittent fasting methods
Intermediate fasting benefits
Dangers of intermittent fasting
Intermittent fasting programs

And, in essence, everything you need to learn how to apply the practice of intermittent fasting to your life program to reap immense intrinsic benefits and thus become a healthier, happier, better and, yes, richer being.

**The Adventures of Sephas (Simple Bedtime Stories for Kids: Quick Read and Illustrations Included):** The Boy who Speaks 100 Languages and Helps Many People All over the World

*It is his 7th birthday, he got a gift. Little did he know what this gift can do for him ... Where will he go? What can he do? Can Sephas save the day?*

*Don't Forget to <u>Claim</u> your FREE ebook!*

# OTHER PROMOTED BOOKS

## S. K. PILGRIM

## I.K. BUTCHER

# KENOSIS BOOKS: BE THE BEST YOU – SELF-IMPROVEMENT SERIES

## SUBSCRIBE AND GET YOUR FREE eBOOK!

If you want to improve the quality of your attention and are willing to do other means to improve your focus and concentration, then this book will definitely help you in that. This book contains the ff:

1. Top Foods to increase your Focus and Concentration
2. Foods you can intake daily to improve your focus
3. Best Juices to Improve your focus
4. Healthy Habits and Eating Style to Improve Focus

..... and much more!

So take action, and scan the QR CODE and/or Subscribe to our **Kenosis Books - Be The Best You: Self-Improvement Series** mailing list and be updated in our latest books and promotions!

# ABOUT THE AUTHOR

S.K. Pilgrim loves nature, travelling, food, and learning. He is a sport buff and loves running a lot. As a marathoner, he believes that keeping himself in good shape not only improves his running but also other aspects of his life. He loves reading books as well as writing them.

S.K. Pilgrim has a full-time job as senior leader in a multinational company. He is very passionate in coaching, training, and organizational development. He never gives up on any talent until they progress and improve to their potential!

Reach SK Pilgrim and our other authors in kenosisbooks@gmail.com Cheers!

# BOOKS BY THIS AUTHOR

GIGA-ENERGY: High Energy Food - Turn-away from Sweets and Energy Drinks BONUS: Low Cholesterol and Low Sugar Energy Boosters

**LOW ON ENERGY? HOW LONG CAN YOU SUSTAIN YOUR ENERGY?**

*Daily tasks and labor require a lot of energy but ending up on the vicious cycle of coffee, sweets, and high-energy drinks is detrimental to our health.*

This book aims to share with you alternative sources of energy that will make you more energetic and last longer through more sustainable and healthy means.

- Instant Energy Boosters
- Long-term Energy Boosters
- Plant-Based Energy Boosters
- Juices and Smoothies Energy Boosters
- Daily Routines to Maintain Energy Levels
- Faster Metabolism and Weight Loss

- Energy-packed Breakfast
- and Much Much More!
- BONUS
    - Low-cholesterol Energy Boosters
    - Low-sugar Energy Boosters

**Grab a copy of this book and let it lead you to GIGA-ENERGY lifestyle!**

# ABOUT THE AUTHOR

I.K. Butcher's passion for building a conducive workplace started when he was in university. He began studying people development and practiced it firsthand. He led teams not only into developing themselves but also directing them into purpose – most especially, the socially oriented one.

Butcher continued this passion when he moved to a consumer goods company after he achieved his university degree. For 12 years, he learned sales, capability building, and business development. He travelled to various places both domestically and internationally to hone his skills and share his lessons to new employees who have begun in their careers.

Butcher believes that one needs to learn multitudes of skills to really excel in an organization and that he is very much willing to share his experiences to help those who are really serious about such an endeavor.

Reach I. K. Butcher and our other authors in kenosisbooks@gmail.com!

# BOOKS BY THIS AUTHOR

MANAGING UPWARDS: THE BEGINNER'S GUIDE IN MANAGING YOUR BOSS (BONUS: THE SOFT SIDE: HOW TO WIN YOUR BOSS BY BUILDING A FRIENDLY RELATIONSHIP)

*Have you been struggling with your boss? Are you a start out with the management skills to workplace excellence? Do you simply fancy the topic and wish to be armed with the artillery for Managing your Boss?*

Whatever the category you find yourself in, this book is poised to arm you with all the necessary strategies for starting and maintaining a healthy and synergistic relationship with your boss in such a way that your personal goals, that of your boss, and the overall objectives of your company are met.

Outlined in well thought of moves, you will be led through four exciting journeys of

✓   Self-identification, skill discovery and skill optimization

✓   Identifying the personal traits, strengths, weaknesses, and context of your boss

✓   Knowing the company, what it stands for, your role and that of your boss

✓   Bridging the gap where stark differences exist

The major chapters all end with action points, step to take to ensure proper use of the information you're provided with. For the young, for the experienced, for whoever seeks to stand out and succeed in the workplace, this is the book for you.

**So, grab a copy now of this book and check out our exciting bonuses and free books that you can avail!**

# Don't Forget to <u>Claim</u> your FREE eBook!

www.ingramcontent.com/pod-product-compliance
Lightning Source LLC
Chambersburg PA
CBHW031550210526
45464CB00003B/1238